MW00680356

PENNSYLVANIA DUTCH
Needlepoint Designs
CHARTED FOR EASY USE

Marcia Loeb

DOVER PUBLICATIONS, INC.
NEW YORK

Published in Canada by General Publishing Company, Ltd., 30 Lesmill Road, Don Mills, Toronto, Ontario.
Published in the United Kingdom by Constable and Company, Ltd., 10 Orange Street, London WC 2.

Pennsylvania Dutch Needlepoint Designs is a new work, first published by Dover Publications in 1976.

International Standard Book Number: 0-486-23299-9
Library of Congress Catalog Card Number: 75-31282

Manufactured in the United States of America
Dover Publications, Inc.
180 Varick Street
New York, N.Y. 10014

INTRODUCTION

The culturally unique Pennsylvania Dutch country is one of America's most attractive and interesting areas. The vibrant folk art of the early German settlers of this area reflects the applications of Old World techniques and traditions to the realities of everyday life in the New. The charming patterns and motifs used to decorate household artifacts have long endeared Pennsylvania Dutch wares to collectors and craftsmen.

This collection of needlepoint designs grew out of my own fascination with the iconography of the "Dutch" country as well as out of an interest in doing needlework. The simple, almost naïve quality of the designs—whether they be a motif from a dower chest, a detail from a ceramic plate or a border from a fractur manuscript—lends itself splendidly to translation into needlepoint.

I have taken my inspiration from many artifacts, including old quilts, samplers, chests, plates, good-conduct drawings, "hex" symbols, birth certificates, textiles and butter molds. I have included many of the most commonly used Pennsylvania Dutch motifs, such as the tulip, the heart, the bird, the urn, the parrot and heavenly figures.

I have made some suggestions on how specific designs might be used, but you should feel free to adapt these motifs to your own projects. You may want to combine several designs, adopting one design as a central motif and creating a border or background out of repeats of another. The Pennsylvania Dutch artisan often painted the date and name of the owner on personal property. Such proof of ownership points to the high value that was placed upon possessions at a time when such things were scarce. I have included a complete alphabet and a set of numerals so that you can personalize your work, if you choose.

Much has been written on what is true Pennsylvania Dutch color. If you examine a number of decorated articles, you will find a great variety of colors and hues. The passage of time has probably dulled the color on some early objects, and the increased availability of color in later years accounts for the wider range of colors used on more recent artifacts. In the needlepoint rendered on the covers I have indicated some of my personal color choices within the framework of what might be considered the traditional Pennsylvania Dutch colors.

It is a good idea to work out a complete, detailed color scheme for the design before beginning a project. You may find it more convenient to put tracing paper over the design and to experiment with colors on the tracing paper. In this way the design in the book will not be ruined if you decide to change the colors.

After you have decided how you want to use your design and have worked out a color scheme, the design may be transferred to the canvas. Since the designs are planned for working on a #10 needlepoint canvas—each square in the grid representing one stitch to be taken on the canvas—the design may be worked directly onto the canvas by counting off on it the same number of warp and woof squares shown in the diagram. You may prefer to outline your design on the canvas itself. Since needlepoint canvas is almost transparent, you can lay it over the designs in the book and trace the pattern directly onto the canvas. If you decide to paint your design onto the canvas, use either a non-soluble ink, acrylic paint thinned appropriately with water so as not to clog the holes in the canvas, or oil paint mixed with benzine or turpentine. Designs placed on the canvas can be colored in as an aid to the worker. Always make sure that your medium is waterproof. Felt tipped pens are very handy both for outlining or coloring in the design on the canvas, but check the labels carefully because not all felt markers are waterproof. Allow all paint to dry thoroughly before beginning any project.

There are two distinct types of needlepoint canvas, single-mesh and double-mesh. Double-mesh is woven with two horizontal and two vertical threads forming each mesh whereas single-mesh is woven with one vertical and one horizontal thread forming each mesh. Double-mesh is a very stable canvas on which the threads will stay securely in place as you work. Single-mesh canvas, which is more widely used, is a little easier on the eyes because the spaces are slightly larger.

A tapestry needle with a rounded, blunt tip and an elongated eye is used for needlepoint. The most commonly used needle for a #10 canvas is the #18 needle. The needle should clear the hole in the canvas without spreading the threads. Special yarns which have good twist and are sufficiently heavy to cover the canvas are used for needlepoint.

Although there are over a hundred different needlepoint stitches, the one that is universally considered to be "the" needlepoint stitch is the *Tent Stitch,* an even, neat stitch that always slants upward from left to right across the canvas. The stitches fit very neatly next to their neighbors and form a hard finish with the distinctive look that belongs to needlepoint. The three most familiar variations of Tent Stitch are: Plain Half-Cross Stitch, Continental Stitch and Basket Weave or Diagonal Stitch. The choice of stitch has a great deal to do with the durability of the finished product.

Plain Half-Cross Stitch, while it does not cover the canvas as well as the other two variations, provides the most economical use of yarn. It uses about one yard of yarn for a square inch of canvas. The stitch works up quickly, but it has a tendency to pull out of shape, a disadvantage that can be corrected in blocking. This stitch should only be used for pictures, wall hangings and areas that will receive little wear. It must be worked on a double-mesh canvas.

Continental Stitch, since it covers the front and back of the canvas, requires more wool than the Plain Half-Cross Stitch (it uses about 1¼ yards of yarn to cover a square inch of fabric). The stitch works up with more thickness on the back than on the front. As a result the piece is more attractive with better wearing ability. This is an ideal stitch for tote bags, belts, headbands, upholstery and rugs since the padding on the reverse saves wear on the needlepoint. The Continental Stitch also pulls the canvas out of shape, but this is easily corrected by blocking.

The Basket Weave or Diagonal Stitch makes an article that is very well padded and will wear well. It uses the same amount of wool as the Continental Stitch and does not pull the canvas out of shape. Since the stitch is actually woven into the canvas, it reinforces the back. This stitch is especially suited for needlepoint projects that will receive a great deal of wear, such as chair seats and rugs. Its disadvantage is that it lacks maneuverability and is hard to do in areas where there are small shapes or intricate designs.

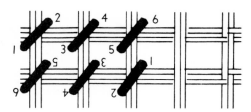

Plain Half-Cross Stitch: Always work Half-Cross Stitch from left to right, then turn the canvas around and work the return row, still stitching from left to right. Bring the needle to the front of the canvas at a point that will be the bottom of the first stitch. The needle is in a vertical position when making the stitch. Keep the stitches loose for minimum distortion and good coverage.

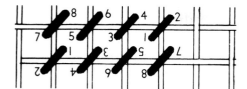

Continental Stitch: Start this design at the upper right-hand corner and work from right to left. The needle is slanted and always brought out a mesh ahead. The resulting stitch is actually a Half-Cross Stitch on top and a slanting stitch on the back. When the row is finished, turn the canvas around and work the return row, still stitching from right to left.

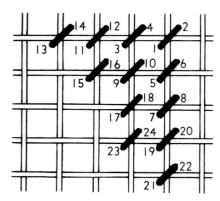

Basket Weave or Diagonal Stitch: Start the Basket Weave in the top right-hand corner *(left-handed workers should begin at the lower left)*. Work the rows diagonally from left to right and then up the canvas from right to left. The rows must be alternated properly or a faint ridge will show where the pattern has been interrupted. Always stop working in the middle of a row rather than at the end so you will know in what direction your are working.

When starting a project, allow at least a 2″ margin of plain canvas around the needlepoint. Bind all the raw edges of the canvas with masking tape, double-fold bias tape or even adhesive tape. There are no set rules on where to begin a design. Generally it is easier to begin close to the center and work outward toward the edges of the canvas, working the backgrounds or borders last. To avoid fraying the yarn, work with strands not longer than 18″.

When you have finished your needlepoint, it should be blocked. No matter how straight you have kept your work, blocking will give it a professional look.

Any hard, flat surface that you do not mind marring with nail holes and one that will not be warped by wet needlepoint can serve as a blocking board. A large piece of plywood, an old drawing board or an old-fashioned doily blocker are ideal.

Moisten a Turkish towel in cold water and roll the needlepoint in the towel. Leaving the needlepoint in the towel overnight will insure that both the canvas and the yarn are thoroughly and evenly dampened. Do not saturate the needlepoint! Never hold the needlepoint under the faucet as this much water is not necessary.

Mark the desired outline on the blocking board, making sure that the corners are straight. Lay the needlepoint on the blocking board, and tack the canvas with thumbtacks about ½″ to ¾″ apart. It will probably take a good deal of pulling and tugging to get the needlepoint straight, but do not be afraid of this stress. Leave the canvas on the blocking board until thoroughly dry. Never put an iron on your needlepoint. You cannot successfully block with a steam iron because the needlepoint must dry in the straightened position. You may also have needlepoint blocked professionally. If you have a pillow made, a picture framed, or chair seat mounted, the craftsman may include the blocking in his price.

Your local needlepoint shop or department where you buy your materials will be happy to help you with any problems.

PENNSYLVANIA DUTCH
Needlepoint Designs

Detail from a dower chest. Suitable for picture, pillow or wall hanging.

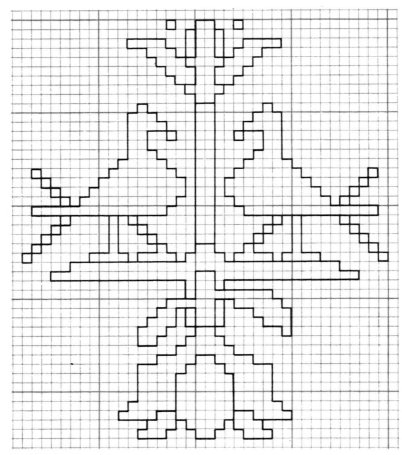

Tulip and bird motif from a needlework sampler. Suitable for small purse or coaster.

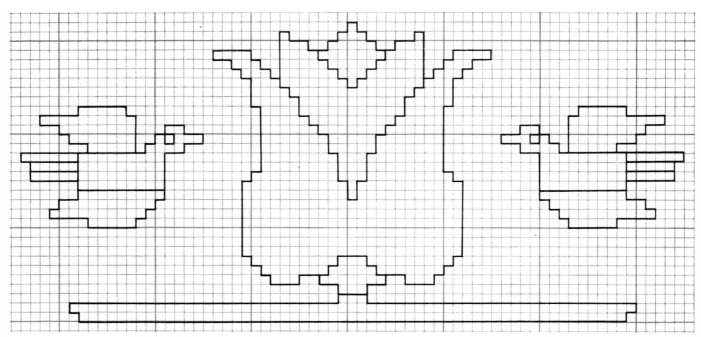

Tulip and bird motif from a ceramic plate. Suitable, as a repeat, for belt or border.

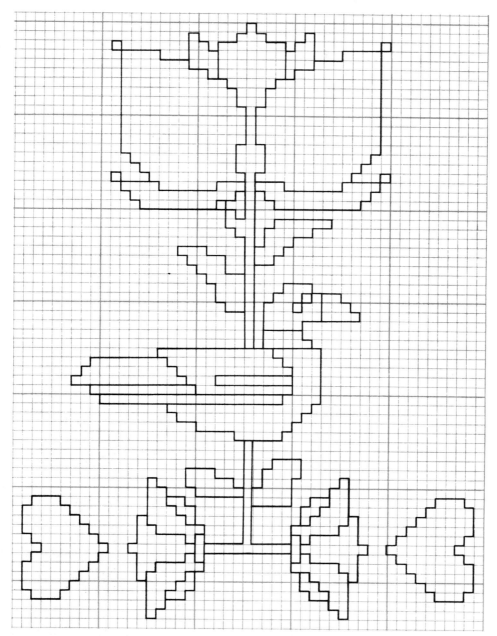

Tulip, bird and heart motif from a needlework sampler. Suitable for pillow or picture.

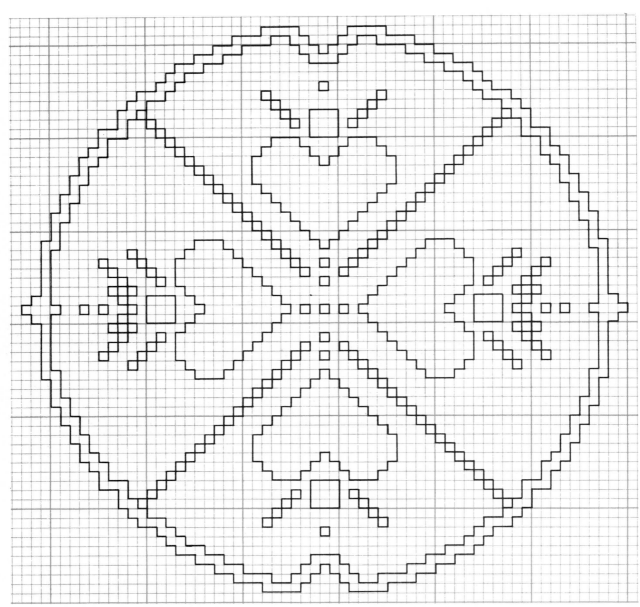

From a design for a quilt block. Suitable for pillow or purse.

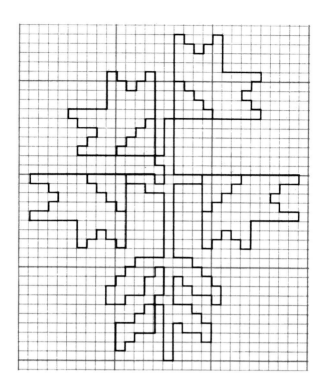

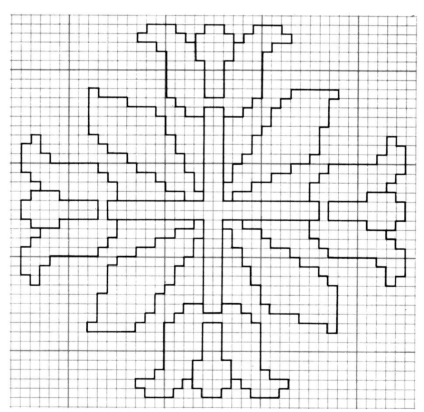

Motifs from appliqué quilts. Suitable for small purses or patches, or, as repeats, for belts or borders.

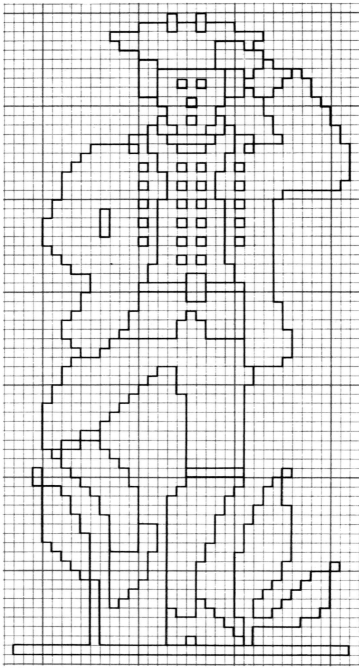

Soldier design from a fractur birth-certificate ("Geburts-Schein"). Suitable for wall hanging or picture.

Angel design from a fractur certificate. Suitable for wall hanging or picture.

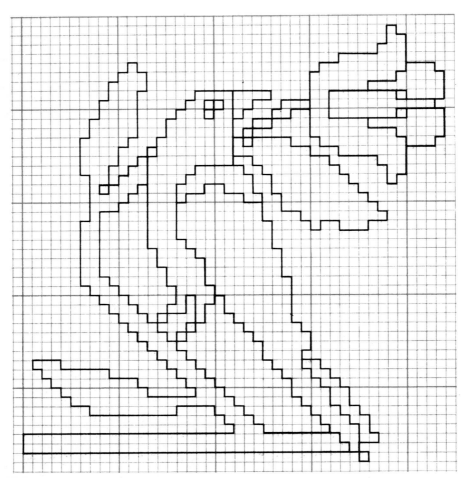

Bird and tulip design from a schoolmaster's good-conduct drawing, called a "reward of merit." Suitable for small pillow, pocket or patch.

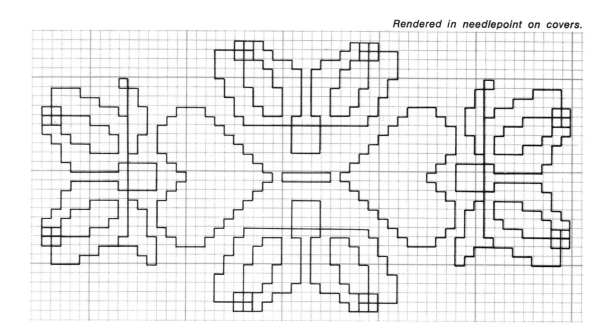

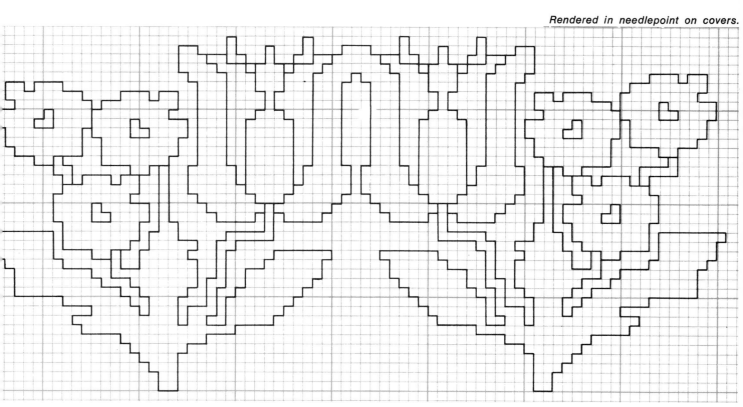

Details from painted chests. Suitable, as repeats, for belts or borders.

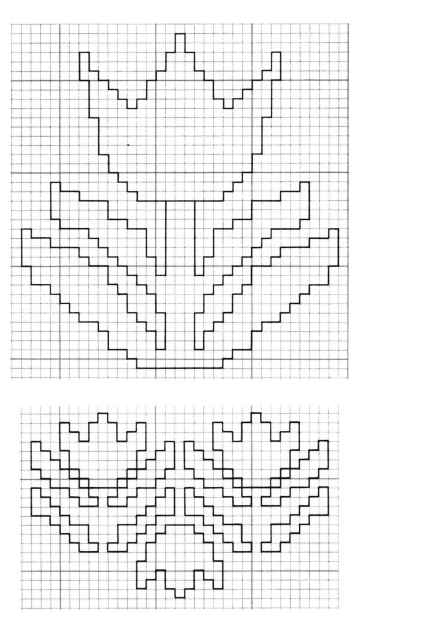

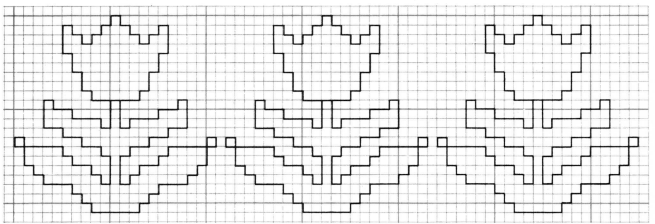

Tulip motifs from appliqué quilt. Suitable for purse, or, as a repeat, for belt or border.

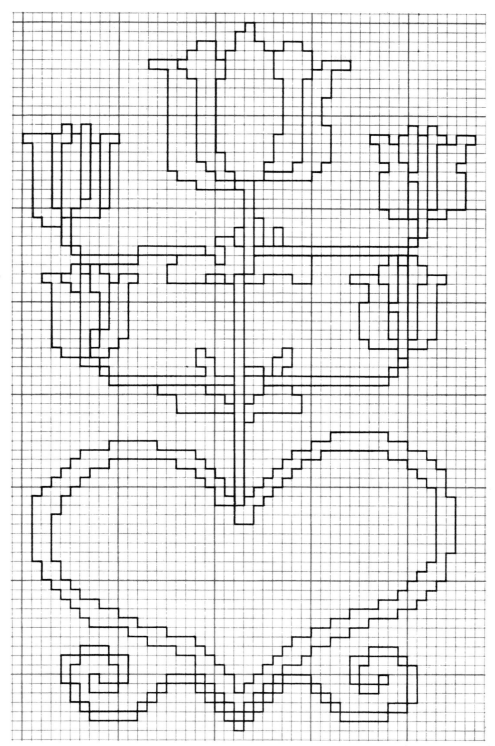

Detail from a fractur drawing. The center of the heart can be filled with initials or dates. Suitable for pillow or wall hanging.

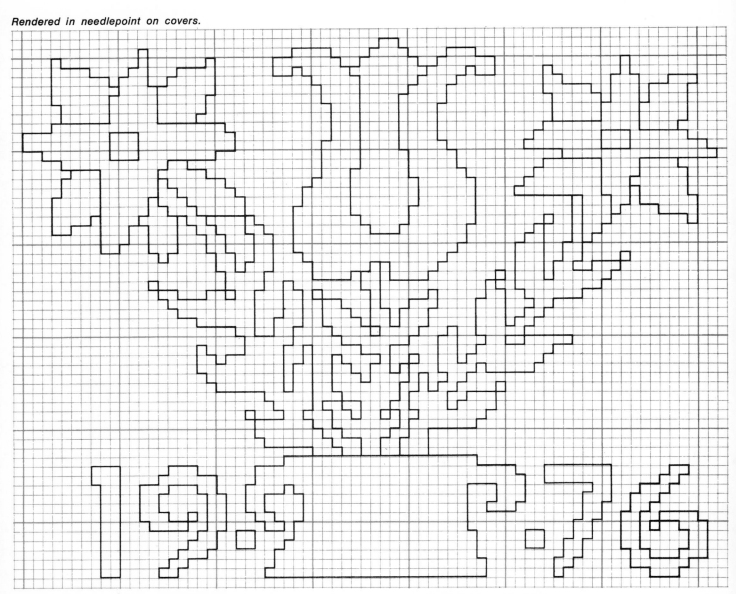

Tulip and urn motif from a dower chest. Suitable for pillow or picture.

George Washington on horseback from a sgraffito ware plate. Suitable for pillow or picture.

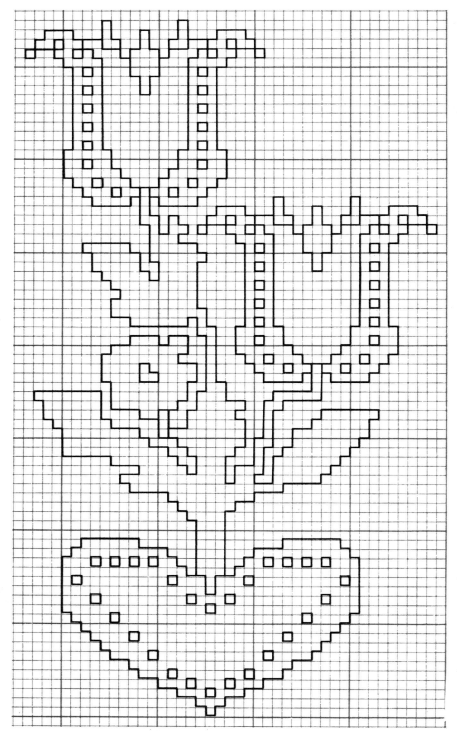

Detail from a dower chest. Suitable for purse or pillow.

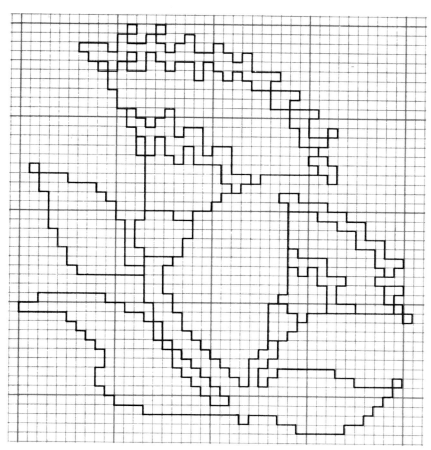

Detail from a painted chest. Suitable for pocket, patch or small purse.

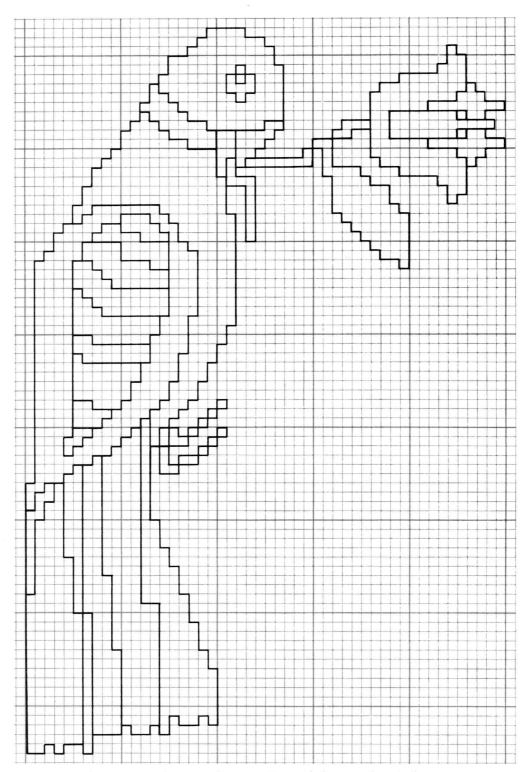

Parrot design from a fractur birth certificate ("Geburts-Schein"). Suitable for wall hanging or tote bag.

Rendered in needlepoint on covers.

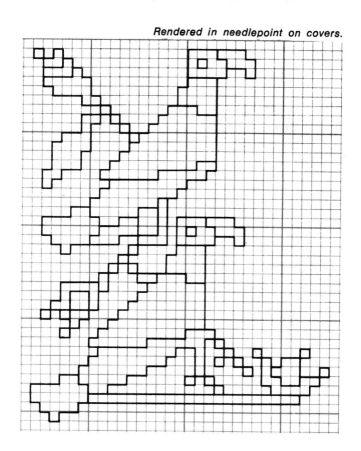

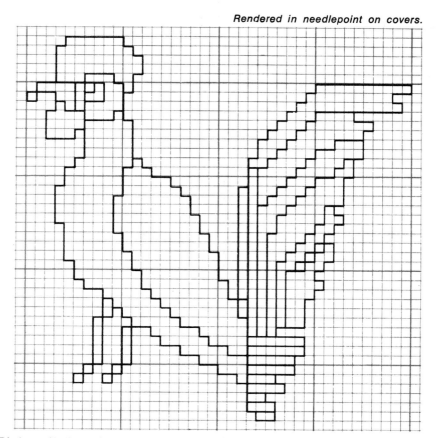

Bird motifs from fractur manuscripts. Suitable for patches or small pillows.

From a design for a quilt block. Suitable for pillow.

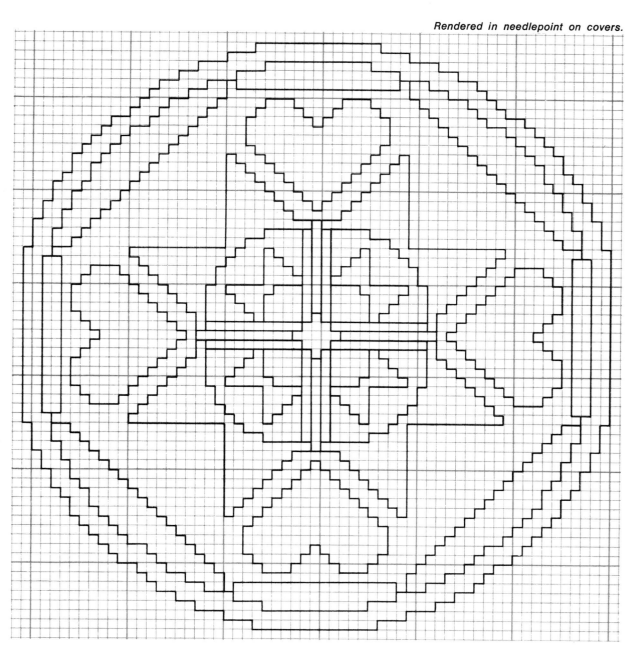

From a design for a quilt block. Suitable for pillow.

Design on a panel of a dower chest. Suitable for pillow or wall hanging.

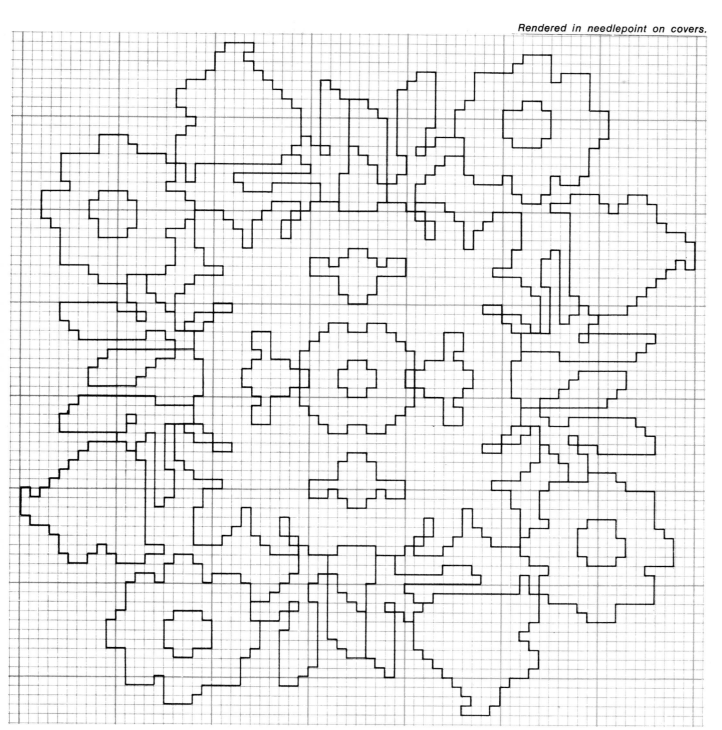

Motif from an appliqué quilt. Suitable for pillow or purse.

Geometric barn sign (commonly called "hex" symbol). Suitable for pillow or purse.

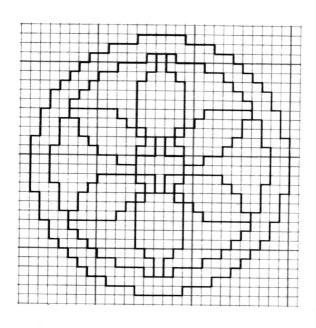

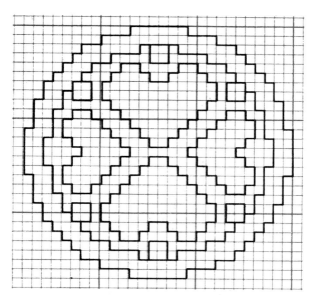

Geometric barn signs (commonly called "hex" symbols). Suitable for patches, pockets or, as repeats, for belts or borders.

Tulip and heart design from a fractur birth certificate ("Geburts-Schein"). Suitable for mirror or picture frame.

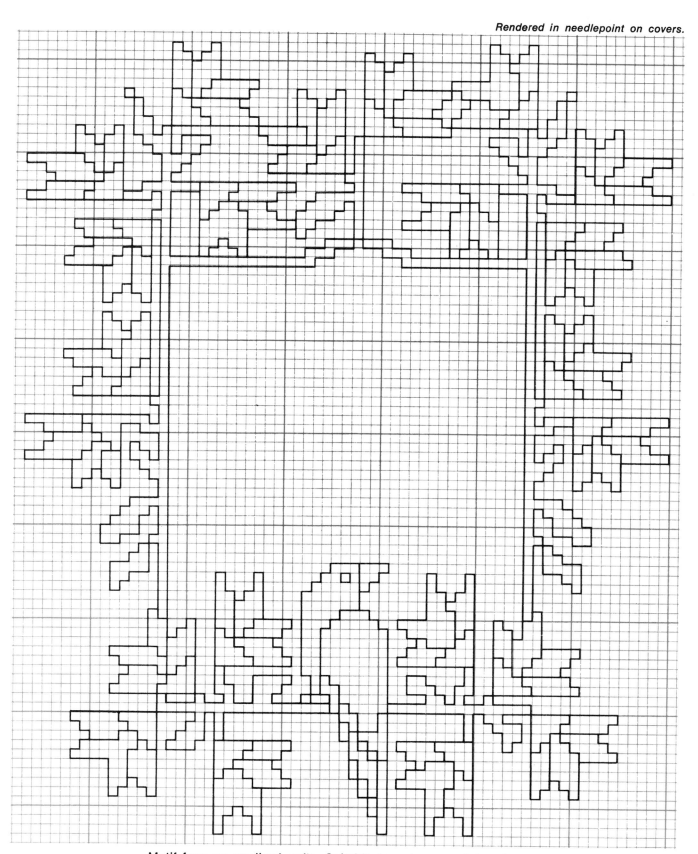

Motif from an appliqué quilt. Suitable for mirror or picture frame.

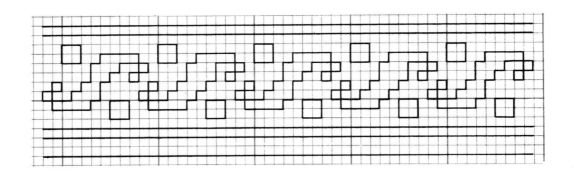

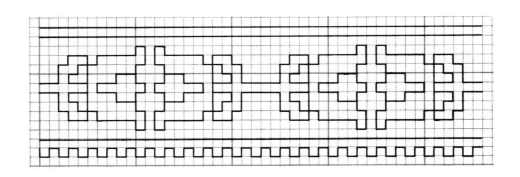

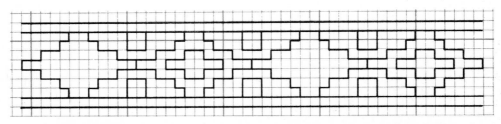

Border designs from textiles. Suitable, as repeats, for belts or borders.

Details from fractur birth certificates ("Geburts-Schein") and baptismal certificates ("Tauf-Schein"). Suitable, as repeats, for belts or borders.

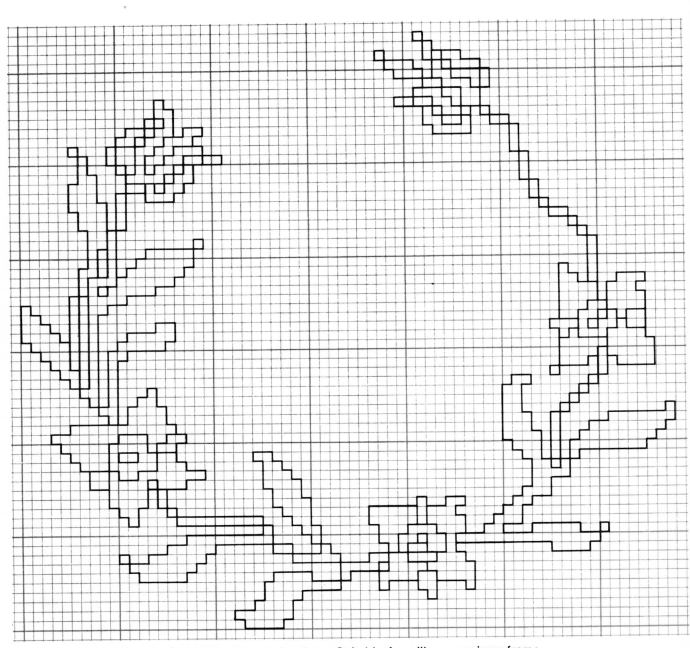

Detail from a ceramic plate. Suitable for pillow or mirror frame.

Bird and flower detail from a painted chest. Suitable for small pillow.

Angel motif from a painted chest. Suitable for small picture.

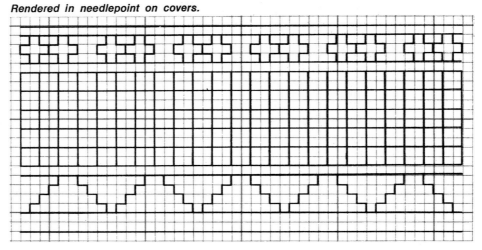

Border design from a fractur manuscript. Suitable, as repeat, for a belt or border.

Fish, tulip and urn motif from an early painted chest. Suitable for wall hanging, pillow or picture.

Motifs from fractur birth certificates ("Geburts-Schein"). Suitable, as repeats, for borders or belts.

Rendered in needlepoint on covers.

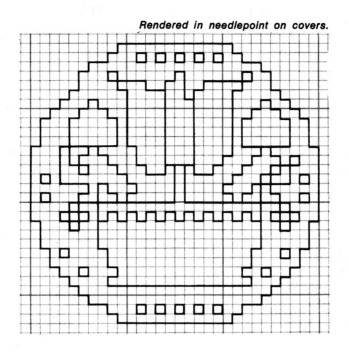

Rendered in needlepoint on covers.

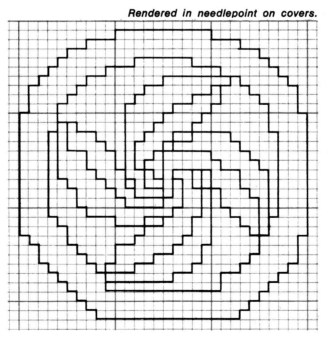

Designs from butter molds. Suitable for small pictures or coasters.

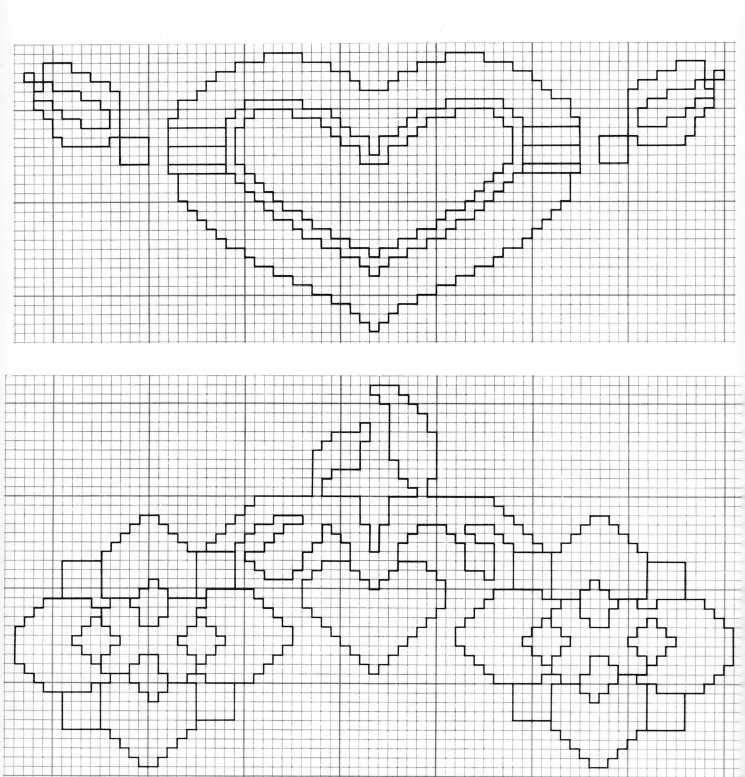

Details from painted furniture. Suitable, as repeats, for borders or belts.

Floral detail from a painted chest. Suitable for pillow, picture or wall hanging.

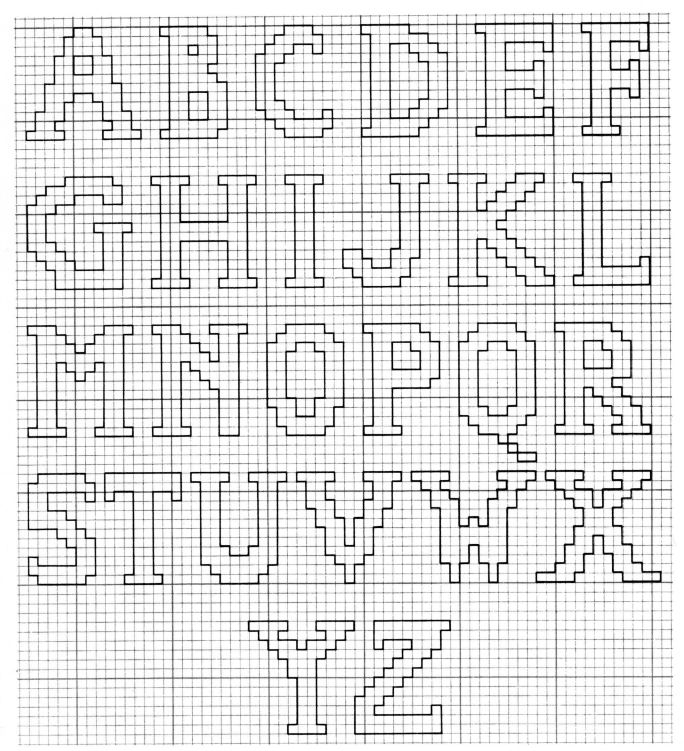

Alphabet to be used in conjunction with other designs.

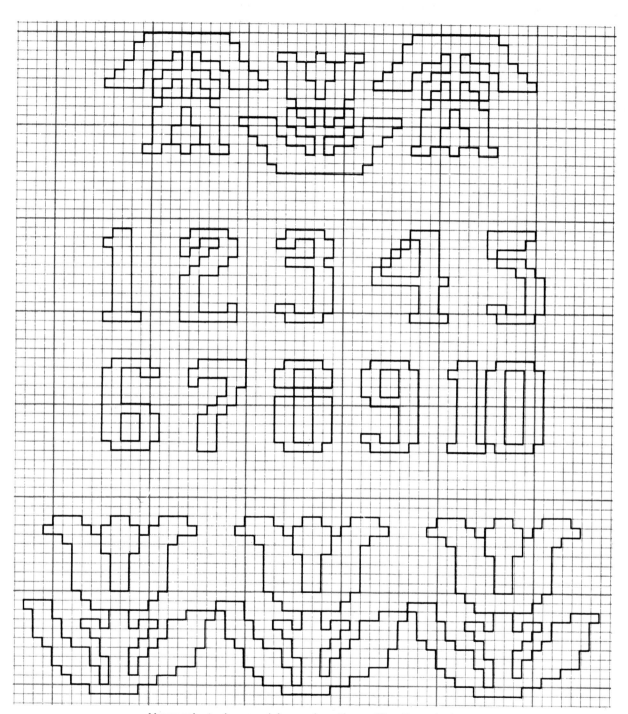

Numerals to be used in conjunction with other designs.

DOVER BOOKS ON NEEDLEPOINT, EMBROIDERY

BASIC NEEDLERY STITCHES ON MESH FABRICS, Mary Ann Beinecke. (21713-2) $3.00

DESIGNS AND PATTERNS FOR EMBROIDERERS AND CRAFTSMEN, Wm. Briggs and Company Ltd. (23030-9) $4.50

HARDANGER EMBROIDERY, Sigrid Bright. (23592-0) $1.50

FRUIT AND VEGETABLE IRON-ON TRANSFER PATTERNS, Barbara Christopher. (23556-4) $1.50

NEEDLEWORK ALPHABETS AND DESIGNS, Blanche Cirker (ed.). (23159-3) $2.25

AMERICAN INDIAN NEEDLEPOINT DESIGNS, Roslyn Epstein. (22973-4) $1.50

DANISH PULLED THREAD EMBROIDERY, Esther Fangel, Ida Winckler and Agnete Madsen. (23474-6) $3.00

PATCHWORK QUILT DESIGNS FOR NEEDLEPOINT, Frank Fontana. (23300-6) $1.50

CHARTED FOLK DESIGNS FOR CROSS-STITCH EMBROIDERY, Maria Foris and Andreas Foris. (23191-7) $2.95

BLACKWORK EMBROIDERY, Elisabeth Geddes and Moyra McNeill. (23245-X) $3.50

VICTORIAN ALPHABETS, MONOGRAMS AND NAMES FOR NEEDLEWORKERS, Godey's Lady's Book. (23072-4) $3.50

VICTORIAN NEEDLEPOINT DESIGNS, Godey's Lady's Book and Peterson's Magazine. (23163-1) $1.75

A TREASURY OF CHARTED DESIGNS FOR NEEDLEWORKERS, Georgia L. Gorham and Jeanne M. Warth. (23558-0) $1.50

GEOMETRIC NEEDLEPOINT DESIGNS, Carol Belanger Grafton. (23160-7) $1.75

FULL-COLOR BICENTENNIAL NEEDLEPOINT DESIGNS, Carol Belanger Grafton. (23233-6) $2.00

FULL-COLOR RUSSIAN FOLK NEEDLEPOINT DESIGNS, Frieda Halpern. (23451-7) $2.25

WHITE WORK: TECHNIQUES AND DESIGNS, Carter Houck (ed.). (23695-1) $1.75

CLASSIC POSTERS FOR NEEDLEPOINT, M. Elizabeth Irvine. (23640-4) $1.50

FAVORITE PETS IN CHARTED DESIGNS, Barbara Johansson. (23889-X) $1.75

CREATIVE STITCHES, Edith John. (22972-6) $3.50

NEW STITCHES FOR NEEDLECRAFT, Edith John. (22971-8) $3.00

PERSIAN RUG MOTIFS FOR NEEDLEPOINT, Lyatif Kerimov. (23187-9) $2.00

CHARTED PEASANT DESIGNS FROM SAXON TRANSYLVANIA, Heinz Kiewe. (23425-8) $2.00

Paperbound unless otherwise indicated. Prices subject to change without notice. Available at your book dealer or write for free catalogues to Dept. Needlework, Dover Publications, Inc., 180 Varick Street, New York, N.Y. 10014. Please indicate field of interest. Each year Dover publishes over 200 books on fine art, music, crafts and needlework, antiques, languages, literature, children's books, chess, cookery, nature, anthropology, science, mathematics, and other areas.

Manufactured in the U.S.A.